CONTENTS

Words that look like <u>this</u> can be found in the glossary on page 24.

LET'S LEARN LIFE CYCLES!

All living things have a life cycle. A life cycle is the stages of growth and change that a living thing goes through. These changes include the beginning of life, growth, reproduction, and death.

Humans begin life as a baby. They grow into a toddler, then a child, and then a teenager. The teenager grows into an adult, who may have babies of their own. Eventually, the adult grows into old age.

MEET THE EARTHWORM

Earthworms are invertebrates. They are burrowing creatures, which means that they spend their time digging into the ground. Earthworms are tube shaped and made up of small ringed segments.

Earthworms are found almost everywhere in the world. They live in many different types of soil. The most common earthworms may be around 3 to 10 inches (8 to 25 cm) long. The longest earthworms can grow over 3 feet (1 m) long.

EGG

The earthworm's life cycle begins with an egg. Earthworm eggs are bunched together inside an egg case called a cocoon. There may be up to 20 eggs inside a single cocoon, depending on the type of earthworm.

Earthworm cocoons are often lemon shaped. The cocoons are left in the soil, where the eggs will hatch after two to four weeks. This can take more or less time depending on the weather.

HATCHLING AND JUVENILE

When the eggs hatch, small but fully formed earthworms emerge. Baby earthworms are called hatchlings. Hatchlings are paler than adult worms. They begin burrowing right away.

Juvenile earthworms look almost exactly like adult earthworms. They have grown to their full size, and their bodies have taken on their proper color. The only body part left for the earthworm to grow is the saddle.

ADULT EARTHWORM

It usually takes around three months for baby earthworms to grow into adults. Juvenile earthworms become adults once they have grown their reproductive organs. This is the thick ring just below an earthworm's head.

Earthworm skin is very special. As well as protecting their insides, it lets out a liquid that helps earthworms move through soil easily. An earthworm's skin also helps it breathe because earthworms do not have lungs.

HOW EARTHWORMS LIVE

The earthworm's body is like a tube within a tube. Its digestive system runs right through its middle, from its mouth to its tail. This is where waste leaves its body.

As earthworms burrow, they pass soil through their digestive system. Their bodies pull out nutrients from the soil before it passes out of its back end. This leaves behind something called worm castings.

Earthworms are hermaphrodites. This means that they have both male and female reproductive organs. This makes it much easier for them to find a mate to reproduce with.

When earthworms mate, the fertilized eggs are held in the saddle. The worm then separates from the saddle. This becomes the protective cocoon for the eggs.

TYPES OF WORMS

It is thought that there are thousands of species of worms in the world. Here is a selection of some of the most interesting ones.

GIANT AFRICAN EARTHWORM

TIGER WORM

has red and yellow stripes

can grow over 3 feet (1 m) long
can mate and make more babies very quickly
EUROPEAN NIGHTCRAWLER
AFRICAN NIGHTCRAWLER
has shiny, dark purple skin

END OF LIFE

As with all living things, an earthworm's life will come to an end. Earthworms usually live between two and seven years. They are often eaten by small creatures such as birds and rodents.

Even though an earthworm dies, as long as it has mated and laid eggs, the life cycle will continue. More worms will hatch from these eggs and continue the cycle.

LIFE CYCLE OF A WORM

An earthworm goes through several changes during its life cycle before it is ready to find a mate and make new earthworms.

An earthworm sheds its saddle, which holds its eggs. This saddle becomes a cocoon, protecting the eggs until a hatchling emerges. It grows into a juvenile, which becomes an adult when it grows its own saddle.

GLOSSARY

digestive system	the parts of the body that work together to break down food
emerge	to become visible by coming out or away from something
fertilized	to do with eggs that have been changed by material from the male of the species
hatch	to break out of an egg
invertebrates	animals without backbones
juvenile	not yet an adult
mate	a partner (of the same species) that an animal chooses to produce young with
nutrients	parts of food that are essential for the body
organs	parts of the body that usually have a specific task
reproduction	making more of the same type of thing
segments	small parts that make up a whole
species	a group of very similar animals or plants that can make babies together

INDEX